JEWISH CEREMONIAL

A GUIDE TO JEWISH PRAYER AND RITUAL

Eli Kellerman

JEWISH CEREMONIAL

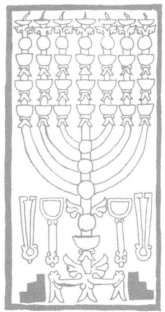

CARTA

Translated by David Maisels

Edited by Moshs Kohn

Published by Carta

ISBN 965-220-038-7
Printed in Israel

Contents

Note: Not all customs are described in this book,
as they vary according to community and locality.

The Life of Man

At five, one is ready to learn
  Scripture
At ten, one is ready to learn
  Mishnah
At thirteen, one is responsible
  for observing the Commandments
At fifteen, one is ready to
  learn Talmud
At eighteen — marriage
At twenty — one's life-pursuit
At thirty — mature strength
At forty — discernment
At fifty — counsel
At sixty — old age
At seventy — grey hairs
At eighty — special strength
At ninety — decrepitude
At a hundred, as though dead and
  gone from the world.

(Sayings of the Fathers 5:24)

הִמּוֹל יִמּוֹל
יְלִיד בֵּיתְךָ
וּמִקְנַת כַּסְפֶּךָ
וְהָיְתָה בְרִיתִי בִּבְשַׂרְכֶם
לִבְרִית עוֹלָם:

Circumcision

"He that is born in thy house, and he that is bought with thy money, must needs be circumcised; and My covenant shall be in your flesh for an everlasting covenant."

(Genesis 17:3)

Circumcision was commanded our father Abraham long before the giving of the Torah. It was intended as a sign upon the flesh of every Jew of the Covenant between the people of Israel and its God. Every father is required to circumcise his son on the eighth day after birth. Since the rite demands medical knowledge and a knowledge of Jewish law, however, it is performed by a professional *mohel* (circumciser) who officiates in place of the father. Circumcision is also required of converts to Judaism.

The man who holds the child on his knees during the ceremony is called a *sandak* (godfather).

The special chair on which the *sandak* sits is called the "throne of Elijah." Elijah is known as the "messenger of the Covenant" because of a legend in the *Zohar*. According to this legend, God commanded Elijah to be present at every circumcision after the prophet had stood before God and accused Israel of "abandoning Thy Covenant."

One of the reasons for having the
circumcision on the eighth day is that the
child should have lived through at least one
Sabbath so that he may enter the Covenant
permeated with its sanctity. Hence the
custom of a "Welcome to the Male"
celebration after the meal on the Sabbath
Eve immediately after the birth of a son.

The Circumcision Ceremony

When the child is brought in to be circumcised, those
present say:

בָּרוּךְ הַבָּא !

Blessed be he that cometh. *(Psalm 118:26)*

The *mohel* says:

אַשְׁרֵי תִּבְחַר וּתְקָרֵב יִשְׁכֹּן חֲצֵרֶיךָ.

Happy is he whom Thou choosest, and
bringest near, that he may dwell in Thy
courts. *(Psalm 65:5)*

Those present respond:

נִשְׂבְּעָה בְּטוּב בֵּיתֶךָ, קְדֹשׁ הֵיכָלֶיךָ.

May we be satisfied with the goodness of
Thy House, even of Thy holy Temple.

(Psalm 65:5)

The father takes the child and says:

אִם אֶשְׁכָּחֵךְ יְרוּשָׁלָיִם תִּשְׁכַּח יְמִינִי :
תִּדְבַּק לְשׁוֹנִי לְחִכִּי אִם לֹא אֶזְכְּרֵכִי
אִם לֹא אַעֲלֶה אֶת יְרוּשָׁלַיִם
עַל רֹאשׁ שִׂמְחָתִי :

If I forget thee, O Jerusalem,
Let my right hand forget her cunning.
Let my tongue cleave to the roof of my
mouth,
If I remember thee not;
If I set not Jerusalem
Above my chiefest joy. *(Psalm 137:5-6)*

11

He continues:

שְׁמַע יִשְׂרָאֵל
יהוה אֱלֹהֵינוּ
יהוה אֶחָד׃

Hear, O Israel,
The Lord our God,
The Lord is One. *(Deuteronomy 6:4)*

This is repeated by those present.

He continues:

יהוה מֶלֶךְ
יהוה מָלָךְ
יהוה יִמְלֹךְ
לְעוֹלָם וָעֶד׃

The Lord reigneth;
The Lord hath reigned;
The Lord shall reign for ever and ever.

This is repeated by those present.

He continues:

אָנָּא יהוה
הוֹשִׁיעָה נָּא׃

Save, we beseech Thee, O Lord!
(Psalm 118:25)

He repeats this, and those present repeat it after him.

Achilles the proselyte explained to his uncle the Roman Emperor Hadrian the meaning of circumcision. Would the emperor, he asked, give a gift to a soldier who had not offered him his allegiance? So the Holy One, Blessed be He does not give His Torah to one who is not circumcised.

He continues:

אָנָּא יהוה הַצְלִיחָה נָא :

We beseech Thee, O Lord, send us prosperity! *(Psalm 118:25)*

He repeats this, and those present repeat it after him.

Sometimes the following is said:

וַיְדַבֵּר יהוה אֶל־מֹשֶׁה לֵּאמֹר :
פִּינְחָס בֶּן־אֶלְעָזָר בֶּן־אַהֲרֹן הַכֹּהֵן
הֵשִׁיב אֶת־חֲמָתִי מֵעַל בְּנֵי־יִשְׂרָאֵל
בְּקַנְאוֹ אֶת־קִנְאָתִי בְּתוֹכָם,
וְלֹא־כִלִּיתִי אֶת־בְּנֵי־יִשְׂרָאֵל בְּקִנְאָתִי :
לָכֵן אֱמֹר, הִנְנִי נֹתֵן לוֹ אֶת־בְּרִיתִי שָׁלוֹם :

And the Lord spoke unto Moses, saying: "Phinehas, the son of Elazar, the son of Aaron the priest, hath turned My wrath away from the children of Israel, in that he was very jealous for My sake amongst them, so that I consumed not the children of Israel in My jealousy. Wherefore I say: Behold, I give unto him My covenant of peace." *(Numbers 25:10-12)*

The child is placed on the throne of Elijah and the *mohel* says:

זֶה הַכִּסֵּא שֶׁל אֵלִיָּהוּ הַנָּבִיא
זָכוּר לַטּוֹב.
לִישׁוּעָתְךָ קִוִּיתִי יהוה :

This is the throne of Elijah,
May he be remembered for good.

I wait for Thy salvation, O Lord.

(Genesis 49:18)

שָׂבַּרְתִּי לִישׁוּעָתְךָ יהוה,
וּמִצְוֹתֶיךָ עָשִׂיתִי:
אֵלִיָּהוּ מַלְאַךְ הַבְּרִית,
הִנֵּה שֶׁלְּךָ לְפָנֶיךָ,
עֲמֹד עַל יְמִינִי וְסָמְכֵנִי.
שָׂבַּרְתִּי לִישׁוּעָתְךָ יהוה.
שָׂשׂ אָנֹכִי עַל אִמְרָתֶךָ
כְּמוֹצֵא שָׁלָל רָב:
שָׁלוֹם רָב לְאֹהֲבֵי תוֹרָתֶךָ
וְאֵין לָמוֹ מִכְשׁוֹל:
אַשְׁרֵי תִּבְחַר וּתְקָרֵב יִשְׁכֹּן חֲצֵרֶיךָ,
נִשְׂבְּעָה בְּטוּב בֵּיתֶךָ קְדֹשׁ הֵיכָלֶךָ:

I have hoped for Thy salvation, O Lord,
And have done Thy commandments.

(Psalm 119:166)

Elijah, messenger of the Covenant,
Behold, he stands before Thee,
Here, beside me at my right hand.
I have hoped for Thy salvation, O Lord,

(Psalm 119:166)

I rejoice at Thy word
As one that finds abundant wealth.

(Psalm 119:162)

Great peace have they who love Thy Torah
And there is no Stumbling for them.

(Psalm 119:165)

Happy is he whom Thou choosest, and
bringest near, that he may dwell in Thy
courts.
May we be satisfied with the goodness of
Thy House, even of Thy holy Temple.

(Psalm 65:5)

The child is placed on the *sandak*'s knees
and the *mohel* says:

בָּרוּךְ אַתָּה יהוה
אֱלֹהֵינוּ מֶלֶךְ הָעוֹלָם,
אֲשֶׁר קִדְּשָׁנוּ בְּמִצְוֹתָיו
וְצִוָּנוּ עַל הַמִּילָה.

Blessed art Thou, O Lord our God,
King of the universe, Who has
sanctified us with His
commandments and commanded us
concerning circumcision.

The *mohel* performs the circumcision.

Immediately after the circumcision, the father says:

בָּרוּךְ אַתָּה יהוה
אֱלֹהֵינוּ מֶלֶךְ הָעוֹלָם,
אֲשֶׁר קִדְּשָׁנוּ בְּמִצְוֹתָיו
וְצִוָּנוּ לְהַכְנִיסוֹ בִּבְרִיתוֹ
שֶׁל אַבְרָהָם אָבִינוּ.

Blessed art Thou, O Lord our God, King of the universe, Who has sanctified us with His commandments and commanded us to bring him into the Covenant of our father Abraham.

בָּרוּךְ אַתָּה יהוה
אֱלֹהֵינוּ מֶלֶךְ הָעוֹלָם,
שֶׁהֶחֱיָנוּ וְקִיְּמָנוּ
וְהִגִּיעָנוּ לַזְּמַן הַזֶּה.

Blessed art Thou, O Lord our God, King of the universe, who has kept us alive, sustained us and brought us to this season.

Those present respond:

אָמֵן.
כְּשֵׁם שֶׁנִּכְנַס לַבְּרִית,
כֵּן יִכָּנֵס
לְתוֹרָה וּלְחֻפָּה
וּלְמַעֲשִׂים טוֹבִים.

Amen. Even as he has entered into the Covenant, so may he enter into the study of Torah, into the wedding-canopy and into a life of good deeds.

15

The *mohel* continues:

בָּרוּךְ אַתָּה יהוה
אֱלֹהֵינוּ מֶלֶךְ הָעוֹלָם,
בּוֹרֵא פְּרִי הַגָּפֶן.

Blessed art Thou, O Lord our God, King of the universe, Who created the fruit of the vine.

בָּרוּךְ אַתָּה יהוה
אֱלֹהֵינוּ מֶלֶךְ הָעוֹלָם,
אֲשֶׁר קִדַּשׁ יְדִיד מִבֶּטֶן,
וְחֹק בִּשְׁאֵרוֹ שָׂם,
וְצֶאֱצָאָיו חָתַם
בְּאוֹת בְּרִית קֹדֶשׁ.
עַל כֵּן בִּשְׂכַר זֹאת,
אֵל חַי חֶלְקֵנוּ צוּרֵנוּ
צַוֵּה לְהַצִּיל
יְדִידוּת שְׁאֵרֵנוּ מִשַּׁחַת,
לְמַעַן בְּרִיתוֹ
אֲשֶׁר בִּבְשָׂרֵנוּ.

Blessed art Thou, O Lord our God, King of the universe, Who sanctified Isaac Thy beloved from the womb, and set Thy Law within his flesh, and sealed his offspring with the sign of Thy holy Covenant. On this account, O living God, our Portion and our Rock, grant that Thy beloved Remnant (Israel) may be saved from destruction, for Thy Covenant's sake that is in our flesh.

16

בָּרוּךְ אַתָּה יהוה
כּוֹרֵת הַבְּרִית.

Blessed art Thou, O Lord, Who made the Covenant.

> Man is not created whole, and it is his duty
> to complete his creation by removal of his
> uncircumcision. In our spiritual nature,
> likewise, we are not created whole, and our
> task is to perfect and complete ourselves
> through continual self-education.

The *mohel* offers up a prayer for the child in which he is formally named:

אֱלֹהֵינוּ וֵאלֹהֵי אֲבוֹתֵינוּ,
קַיֵּם אֶת הַיֶּלֶד הַזֶּה לְאָבִיו וּלְאִמּוֹ,
וְיִקָּרֵא שְׁמוֹ בְּיִשְׂרָאֵל (פלוני בן פלוני).
יִשְׂמַח הָאָב בְּיוֹצֵא חֲלָצָיו
וְתָגֵל אִמּוֹ בִּפְרִי בִטְנָהּ,
כַּכָּתוּב: יִשְׂמַח אָבִיךָ וְאִמֶּךָ
וְתָגֵל יוֹלַדְתֶּךָ:
וְנֶאֱמַר: וָאֶעֱבֹר עָלַיִךְ
וָאֶרְאֵךְ מִתְבּוֹסֶסֶת בְּדָמָיִךְ,
וָאֹמַר לָךְ בְּדָמַיִךְ חֲיִי,
וָאֹמַר לָךְ בְּדָמַיִךְ חֲיִי:

Our God and God of our fathers,
Preserve this child to his father and mother,
And may his name in Israel be ... son of...
May his father rejoice in the offspring of his loins
And his mother in the fruit of her womb,
As it is written: "Thy father and mother shall rejoice,
And her that bare thee be glad *(Proverbs 23:25)*
And it is said: "And when I passed by thee, I saw thee weltering in thy blood,
And I said to thee, 'In thy blood live.'
And I said to thee: 'In thy blood live.'"

(Ezekiel 16:6)

Sometimes the *mohel* dips his finger in wine at this point, and places it on the child's lips.

17

He continues:

וְנֶאֱמַר : זָכַר לְעוֹלָם בְּרִיתוֹ,
דָּבָר צִוָּה לְאֶלֶף דּוֹר :
אֲשֶׁר כָּרַת אֶת אַבְרָהָם
וּשְׁבוּעָתוֹ לְיִשְׂחָק :
וַיַּעֲמִידֶהָ לְיַעֲקֹב לְחֹק,
לְיִשְׂרָאֵל בְּרִית עוֹלָם :
וְנֶאֱמַר : וַיָּמָל אַבְרָהָם אֶת יִצְחָק
בְּנוֹ בֶּן שְׁמוֹנַת יָמִים,
כַּאֲשֶׁר צִוָּה אֹתוֹ אֱלֹהִים :
הוֹדוּ לַיהוה כִּי טוֹב,
כִּי לְעוֹלָם חַסְדּוֹ :

And it is said, He hath remembered His Covenant for ever,
The word which He hath commanded for a thousand generations;
The Covenant which He hath made with Abraham,
And His oath unto Isaac.
He confirmed it unto Jacob for a law,
Unto Israel for an everlasting Covenant. *(Psalm 105:8-10)*
And it is said: And Abraham circumcised his son Isaac
When he was eight days old,
As God had commanded him. *(Genesis 21:4)*
O give thanks unto the Lord, for He is good,
For His mercy endureth for ever. *(Psalm 118:1)*

Those present repeat:

הוֹדוּ לַיהוה כִּי טוֹב,
כִּי לְעוֹלָם חַסְדּוֹ :

O give thanks unto the Lord, for He is good,
For His mercy endureth for ever.

(Psalm 118:1)

He continues:

(פלוני) זֶה הַקָּטֹן גָּדוֹל יִהְיֶה.
כְּשֵׁם שֶׁנִּכְנַס לַבְּרִית,
כֵּן יִכָּנֵס לְתוֹרָה וּלְחֻפָּה
וּלְמַעֲשִׂים טוֹבִים. אָמֵן.

May this little child (name) grow to manhood.
Even as he has entered into the Covenant, so may he enter into the study of Torah, into the wedding-canopy and into a life of good deeds.

The *mohel* drinks some wine and places a little on the child's lips.

The
Redemption
of the
Firstborn

קַדֶּשׁ־לִי כָל־בְּכוֹר
פֶּטֶר כָּל־רֶחֶם
בִּבְנֵי יִשְׂרָאֵל
בָּאָדָם וּבַבְּהֵמָה
לִי הוּא :

"Sanctify unto Me all the firstborn, whatsoever openeth the womb among the children of Israel, both of man and beast: it is Mine."

(Exodus 13:2)

Even before the Exodus from Egypt, after the slaying of the firstborn, the firstborn sons of Israel were sanctified to God. This sanctification found its concrete expression in the Biblical commandment to redeem every firstborn son to his mother. The redemption of the firstborn takes place 31 days after birth when, according to Jewish law, his survival is regarded as assured. If one of the parents is a Cohen or a Levite, they are exempt from the requirement to redeem their son, for the tribe of Levi is a special category—sanctified to God in its entirety.

The child is redeemed by giving five silver shekels or an article of that value to the Cohen (priest). (The value of the five silver shekels referred to in the Bible changes in relation to the value of the coins. The State of Israel has minted special coins for use in the Redemption ceremony.)

> *"The earth is the Lord's and the fullness thereof."* *(Psalm 24:1)*
> *The whole world and all that is in it belongs to God. Thus, everything we enjoy in the world must first be offered up to God to remind us that what we enjoy is not our own. This is why they offered up the first of the crops and the first fruits, the first of the fleeces, the first of the sheep and the firstborn of mankind.*

The Redemption Ceremony

The Redemption ceremony generally takes place in the course of a festive meal in honour of the occasion. When the meal has begun, the child is brought in, and the father takes him to the priest and says:

זֶה בְּנִי בְכוֹרִי
וְהוּא פֶּטֶר רֶחֶם לְאִמּוֹ.
וְהַקָּדוֹשׁ בָּרוּךְ הוּא צִוָּה לִפְדּוֹתוֹ
שֶׁנֶּאֱמַר: "וּפְדוּיָו מִבֶּן־חֹדֶשׁ תִּפְדֶּה
בְּעֶרְכְּךָ כֶּסֶף חֲמֵשֶׁת שְׁקָלִים בְּשֶׁקֶל
הַקֹּדֶשׁ עֶשְׂרִים גֵּרָה הוּא".

This my firstborn son is the firstborn of his mother, and the Holy One, Blessed be He has commanded to redeem him, as it is said: "And those that are to be redeemed of them from a month old shalt thou redeem, according to thine estimation, for the money of five shekels, after the shekel of the sanctuary, which is twenty gerahs." *(Numbers 18:16)*

The priest asks:

אֵיזֶה תִּרְצֶה יוֹתֵר,
בִּנְךָ בְכוֹרְךָ זֶה,
אוֹ חֲמִשָּׁה סְלָעִים
שֶׁנִּתְחַיַּבְתָּ בְּפִדְיוֹנוֹ?

Which would you rather, give me your firstborn son, or pay the five shekels required for his redemption?

22

The father answers:

חָפֵץ אֲנִי לִפְדּוֹת אֶת בְּנִי,
וְהֵא לְךָ דְּמֵי פִּדְיוֹנוֹ
שֶׁנִּתְחַיַּבְתִּי מִן הַתּוֹרָה.

I would rather redeem my son, and here is his redemption-price as required by the Torah.

The father takes the money or the article which he will give to the priest, and says:

בָּרוּךְ אַתָּה יהוה
אֱלֹהֵינוּ מֶלֶךְ הָעוֹלָם,
אֲשֶׁר קִדְּשָׁנוּ בְּמִצְוֹתָיו
וְצִוָּנוּ עַל פִּדְיוֹן הַבֵּן.

Blessed art Thou, O Lord our God, King of the universe, Who has sanctified us with His commandments and commanded us concerning the Redemption of the Firstborn.

בָּרוּךְ אַתָּה יהוה
אֱלֹהֵינוּ מֶלֶךְ הָעוֹלָם,
שֶׁהֶחֱיָנוּ וְקִיְּמָנוּ
וְהִגִּיעָנוּ לַזְּמַן הַזֶּה.

Blessed art Thou, O Lord our God, King of the universe, Who has kept us alive, sustained us and brought us to this season.

The father gives the priest the redemption-money:

The priest lays his hand on the child's head and says:

יְשִׂמְךָ אֱלֹהִים
כְּאֶפְרַיִם וְכִמְנַשֶּׁה :

God make thee
As Ephraim and Manasseh.

(Genesis 48:20)

> *Originally, the firstborn sons constituted the priesthood amongst the people, and they offered up the sacrifices. But because they were involved in the worship of the golden calf, God withdrew the priesthood from them and gave it to the tribe of Levi, which had no part in this idolatry. Through the Redemption of the Firstborn, the sanctity is transferred from the firstborn son to the priest (a member of the tribe of Levi) who receives the Redemption payment.*

יְבָרֶכְךָ יהוה וְיִשְׁמְרֶךָ :
יָאֵר יהוה פָּנָיו
אֵלֶיךָ וִיחֻנֶּךָּ :
יִשָּׂא יהוה פָּנָיו אֵלֶיךָ
וְיָשֵׂם לְךָ שָׁלוֹם :
יהוה שֹׁמְרֶךָ
יהוה צִלְּךָ עַל־יַד יְמִינֶךָ :

The Lord bless thee, and keep thee:
The Lord make His face to shine upon thee,
And be gracious unto thee:
The Lord lift up His countenance upon thee,
And give thee peace.   *(Numbers 6:24)*
The Lord is thy keeper:
The Lord is thy shade upon thy right hand.   *(Psalm 121:5)*

24

יהוה יִשְׁמָרְךָ מִכָּל־רָע
יִשְׁמֹר אֶת־נַפְשֶׁךָ :
כִּי אֹרֶךְ יָמִים וּשְׁנוֹת חַיִּים
וְשָׁלוֹם יוֹסִיפוּ לָךְ :

The Lord shall guard thee from all ill;
He shall preserve thy soul.

(Psalm 121:7)

For length of days, and long life,
And peace shall they add to thee.

(Proverbs 3:2)

The priest takes a cup of wine, and says:

בָּרוּךְ אַתָּה יהוה
אֱלֹהֵינוּ מֶלֶךְ הָעוֹלָם
בּוֹרֵא פְּרִי הַגָּפֶן.

Blessed art Thou, O Lord our God,
King of the universe, Who created
the fruit of the vine.

בֶּן
שְׁלֹשׁ עֶשְׂרֵה
לְמִצְוֹת;

Bar Mitzvah

*At thirteen, one is responsible for
observing the Commandments*
(Sayings of the Fathers 5:24)

A boy who has reached the age of thirteen years and a day (and a girl, twelve years and a day) is considered "adult" according to Jewish law, responsible for his actions and liable for punishment. From that age he is required to perform all the commandments (such as laying on phylacteries, observing the five fasts, etc.), even if previously he had performed only some of them voluntarily as part of his education. Such a boy began to be called *bar mitzvah* ("son of the commandment") in about the 14th century. About that time the custom developed of marking this coming-of-age in public with a great celebration—a custom that is still observed. On the first Sabbath after reaching his thirteenth year a boy is called to the Torah in the synagogue, where he will read part of the weekly portion from the Torah or the Prophets, according to his abilities. In some cases the rabbi makes a speech in honour of the boy. The event generally includes a ceremonial meal at which the boy makes a speech on a subject from the Torah related to the occasion.

The *bat mitzvah* celebration for a girl is a much later custom. This was usually a far less public occasion, confined to the family circle. Recently, the custom has developed of celebrating the *bat mitzvah,* too, with a festive meal.

The Reading of the Torah

The custom of reading the Torah on fixed days of the week is ancient dating back to the time of Ezra, and from an early period was established in religious law. Every Sabbath the weekly "portion"—a section of the Torah—is read, and at every festival a section of the Torah connected with that festival. Every Monday and Thursday, moreover, a short passage is read from the beginning of the weekly portion, so that a Jew will not allow three days to go by without reading the Torah.

In former times the weekly portion was divided out among several persons each of whom was called up to the platform to read a section of it. Nowadays, however, when fewer people are able to read the Torah, one man is appointed to read it aloud, and the man called to the reading accompanies him softly and says only the blessings aloud. The number of those called to the Torah varies according to the importance of the occasion, but the first three are always a Cohen, a Levite and a Jew in neither category—in that order. After the conclusion of the reading, on Sabbaths and festivals, a portion from the Prophets (the *Haftarah*) is read, related to the subject of the weekly portion.

The Ceremony of Reading the Torah

The person called to the Torah looks at the place where the reader is about to begin, and says:

בָּרְכוּ אֶת יהוה הַמְבֹרָךְ.

Bless the Lord Who is to be blessed.

The congregation responds:

בָּרוּךְ יהוה הַמְבֹרָךְ לְעוֹלָם וָעֶד.

Blessed be the Lord Who is to be blessed, for ever and ever.

He repeats:

בָּרוּךְ יהוה הַמְבֹרָךְ לְעוֹלָם וָעֶד.

Blessed be the Lord Who is to be blessed, for ever and ever.

29

He continues:

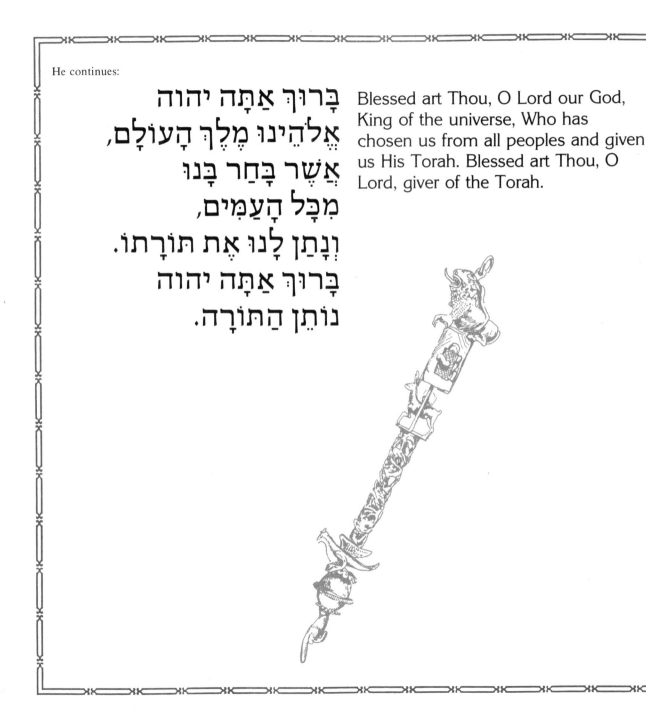

בָּרוּךְ אַתָּה יהוה
אֱלֹהֵינוּ מֶלֶךְ הָעוֹלָם,
אֲשֶׁר בָּחַר בָּנוּ
מִכָּל הָעַמִּים,
וְנָתַן לָנוּ אֶת תּוֹרָתוֹ.
בָּרוּךְ אַתָּה יהוה
נוֹתֵן הַתּוֹרָה.

Blessed art Thou, O Lord our God, King of the universe, Who has chosen us from all peoples and given us His Torah. Blessed art Thou, O Lord, giver of the Torah.

The reader reads aloud, and the person called to the Torah accompanies him softly. On conclusion of the reading of the passage, the latter says:

בָּרוּךְ אַתָּה יהוה
אֱלֹהֵינוּ מֶלֶךְ הָעוֹלָם,
אֲשֶׁר נָתַן לָנוּ תּוֹרַת אֱמֶת
וְחַיֵּי עוֹלָם נָטַע בְּתוֹכֵנוּ.
בָּרוּךְ אַתָּה יהוה
נוֹתֵן הַתּוֹרָה.

Blessed art Thou, O Lord our God, King of the universe, Who has given us the Torah of truth and planted everlasting life in our midst. Blessed art Thou, O Lord, Who has given us the Torah.

After this blessing, the father of a *bar mitzvah* who has been called to the Torah for the first time says:

בָּרוּךְ שֶׁפְּטָרַנִי מֵעָנְשׁוֹ שֶׁלָּזֶה.

Blessed be He who has relieved me of responsibility for this one's sins.

If the person called to the Torah has just recovered from a serious illness or escaped danger, he says:

בָּרוּךְ אַתָּה יהוה
אֱלֹהֵינוּ מֶלֶךְ הָעוֹלָם,
הַגּוֹמֵל לְחַיָּבִים טוֹבוֹת,
שֶׁגְּמָלַנִי כָּל טוֹב.

Blessed art Thou, O Lord our God, King of the universe, Who does good to the undeserving, for dealing kindly with me.

The congregation responds:

אָמֵן. מִי שֶׁגְּמָלְךָ כָּל טוֹב
הוּא יִגְמָלְךָ כָּל טוֹב, סֶלָה.

Amen. May He Who has shown you every kindness deal kindly with you for ever.

31

The Weekly Portions

On the festival of *Simhat Torah* (the Celebration of the Torah) — the eighth day of the feast of *Succot* (Tabernacles) — the reading of the Torah is concluded with the portion *Vezot haberakha* ("And this is the blessing"), and on the same day a new reading is begun with the opening portion of Genesis: *Bereshit* ("In the beginning"). On most Sabbaths, only one portion is read, but sometimes two are read in order that the reading of the final portion will always fall on *Simhat Torah* (the number of Sabbaths being different each year). It is the practice to begin the reading of the book of Exodus in the second half of the month of Tevet, Leviticus between Purim and Passover, Numbers at the end of the month of Iyar or at the beginning of Sivan (before the feast of Shavuot), and Deuteronomy before the fast of Tisha B'Av.

Genesis	Exodus	Leviticus	Numbers	Deuteronomy
Bereshit	*Shemot*	*Vayikra*	*Bamidbar*	*Devarim*
Noah	*Va'era*	*Tsav*	*Nasso*	*Va'et'hanan*
Lekh-lekha	*Bo*	*Shemini*	*Beha'alotekha*	*Ekev*
Vayera	*Beshalah*	*Tazria*	*Shelah*	*Re'ei*
Hayei Sara	*Yitro*	*Metsora*	*Korah*	*Shofetim*
Toledot	*Mishpatim*	*Aharei mot*	*Hukat*	*Ki tetsei*
Vayetsei	*Truma*	*Kedoshim*	*Balak*	*Ki tavo*
Vayishlah	*Tetsaveh*	*Emor*	*Pinhas*	*Nitsavim*
Vayeshev	*Ki tissa*	*Behar*	*Matot*	*Vayelekh*
Mikets	*Vayak'hel*	*Behukotai*	*Masei*	*Ha'azinu*
Vayigash	*Pekudei*			*Vezot haberakha*
Vayehi				

Marriage

וַיְבָ֣רֶךְ אֹתָם֮ אֱלֹהִים֒
וַיֹּ֨אמֶר לָהֶ֜ם אֱלֹהִ֗ים
פְּר֣וּ וּרְב֤וּ
וּמִלְא֥וּ אֶת־הָאָ֖רֶץ
וְכִבְשֻׁ֑הָ ׃

"And God blessed them, and God said unto them: 'Be fruitful, and multiply, and replenish the earth, and subdue it.'" (Genesis 1:28)

The union of man and woman for the purpose of creating a family is a prerequisite for the fulfillment of the first commandment given in the Torah — "Be fruitful, and multiply and replenish the earth." In Jewish law this union is seen as a sacred matter: the man consecrates the woman, i.e., separates her and raises her above other women, and the woman is sanctified to her husband and forbidden to others.

In the Talmudic period this sanctification of the woman took place in two stages. The first stage was the betrothal or *kiddushin*, in which the man gave the woman an article worth one prutah and sanctified her by saying, "Behold, thou art consecrated" etc., and by the betrothal blessing. The betrothal was accompanied by a festive meal. The wedding took place some time afterwards, generally twelve months later. The two sides drew up the *ketubah* (marriage contract), which specifies the obligations of a husband to his wife, and the groom gave the document to his bride. The six marriage blessings were read out, and the bride was taken to the bridegroom's house with great joy. On her wedding day the bride covered her hair, because a married woman was not allowed to reveal her hair in public.

Nowadays, the two ceremonies are combined, and the betrothal and the wedding take place successively under the *huppah* (wedding canopy).

It is usual for the bride and bridegroom to fast on their wedding day. The day is like a private Yom Kippur (Day of Atonement) when their sins are forgiven.

The Wedding Ceremony

The bridegroom goes up to the bride where she is sitting and covers her face with a veil. Those present say:

אֲחֹתֵנוּ אַתְּ הֲיִי לְאַלְפֵי רְבָבָה.

Our sister, may thou be mother of thousands of myriads! *(Genesis 24:60)*

The wedding ceremony is customarily held out of doors, because it is written: "I will multiply thy seed as the stars of heaven."
(Genesis 22:17)

The bridegroom is escorted to the *huppah*, and then the bride is brought to him. The rabbi takes a cup of wine and says:

בָּרוּךְ אַתָּה יהוה
אֱלֹהֵינוּ מֶלֶךְ הָעוֹלָם,
בּוֹרֵא פְּרִי הַגָּפֶן.

Blessed art Thou, O Lord our God, King of the universe, Who created the fruit of the vine.

He then says the betrothal blessing:

בָּרוּךְ אַתָּה יהוה
אֱלֹהֵינוּ מֶלֶךְ הָעוֹלָם,
אֲשֶׁר קִדְּשָׁנוּ בְּמִצְוֹתָיו
וְצִוָּנוּ עַל הָעֲרָיוֹת,
וְאָסַר לָנוּ אֶת הָאֲרוּסוֹת,
וְהִתִּיר לָנוּ
אֶת הַנְּשׂוּאוֹת לָנוּ
עַל יְדֵי חֻפָּה וְקִדּוּשִׁין.
בָּרוּךְ אַתָּה יהוה
מְקַדֵּשׁ עַמּוֹ יִשְׂרָאֵל
עַל יְדֵי חֻפָּה וְקִדּוּשִׁין.

Blessed art Thou, O Lord our God, King of the universe, Who has sanctified us with His commandments and commanded us concerning forbidden unions. He has debarred from us those who are betrothed, but sanctioned us those who are married to us by the *huppah* and the sacred covenant of wedlock.

Blessed art Thou, O Lord, Who sanctifies His people Israel through the *huppah* and the sacred covenant of wedlock.

The bridegroom and bride drink from the cup of wine.

The groom produces the ring and testifies before two witnesses that it is his. He places it on the forefinger of the right hand of the bride, and says:

הֲרֵי אַתְּ מְקֻדֶּשֶׁת לִי בְּטַבַּעַת זוֹ כְּדַת משֶׁה וְיִשְׂרָאֵל.

Behold, thou art consecrated unto me by this ring according to the law of Moses and of Israel.

The bridegroom crushes a glass underfoot as a reminder of the desctruction of the Temple.

> *In the* Gemara, *the story is told of the breaking of an expensive glass at the time of the* huppah *so as to moderate the joy, which would then have reached its climax, in order to prevent the joy of the sacred occasion from turning into wild revelry.*

The rabbi reads out the *ketubah* (marriage contract) and hands it to the groom to give to the bride.

After the bride has received the *ketubah*, the rabbi pronounces the seven marriage blessings, beginning with a blessing over a second cup of wine:

בָּרוּךְ אַתָּה יהוה אֱלֹהֵינוּ מֶלֶךְ הָעוֹלָם, בּוֹרֵא פְּרִי הַגָּפֶן.

Blessed art Thou, O Lord our God, King of the universe, Who created the fruit of the vine.

The rabbi continues:

בָּרוּךְ אַתָּה יהוה
אֱלֹהֵינוּ מֶלֶךְ הָעוֹלָם,
שֶׁהַכֹּל בָּרָא לִכְבוֹדוֹ.

Blessed art Thou, O Lord our God, King of the universe, Who created all things for His glory.

בָּרוּךְ אַתָּה יהוה
אֱלֹהֵינוּ מֶלֶךְ הָעוֹלָם,
יוֹצֵר הָאָדָם.

Blessed art Thou, O Lord our God, King of the universe, Who created Man.

בָּרוּךְ אַתָּה יהוה
אֱלֹהֵינוּ מֶלֶךְ הָעוֹלָם,
אֲשֶׁר יָצַר
אֶת הָאָדָם בְּצַלְמוֹ
בְּצֶלֶם דְּמוּת תַּבְנִיתוֹ,
וְהִתְקִין לוֹ מִמֶּנּוּ
בִּנְיַן עֲדֵי עַד.
בָּרוּךְ אַתָּה יהוה
יוֹצֵר הָאָדָם.

Blessed art Thou, O Lord our God, King of the universe, Who made man in His image, in His very likeness, and created woman out of him to be at his side for ever. Blessed art Thou, O Lord, Who created Man.

שׂוֹשׂ תָּשִׂישׂ
וְתָגֵל הָעֲקָרָה
בְּקִבּוּץ בָּנֶיהָ
לְתוֹכָהּ בְּשִׂמְחָה.
בָּרוּךְ אַתָּה יהוה
מְשַׂמֵּחַ צִיּוֹן בְּבָנֶיהָ.

May she who was barren (Zion) exult and be glad when her children are gathered within her in joy. Blessed art Thou, O Lord, Who causes Zion to rejoice in her children.

In admonishing husbands to be careful to treat their wives with respect, the Talmudic Sages taught that a man ought to honour his wife more than his own flesh.

שַׂמֵּחַ תְּשַׂמַּח
רֵעִים הָאֲהוּבִים
כְּשַׂמֵּחֲךָ יְצִירְךָ
בְּגַן עֵדֶן מִקֶּדֶם.
בָּרוּךְ אַתָּה יהוה
מְשַׂמֵּחַ חָתָן וְכַלָּה.

O delight these loved companions, as once Thou didst gladden Thy creation in the garden of Eden. Blessed art Thou, O Lord, who causes the bridegroom and the bride to rejoice.

בָּרוּךְ אַתָּה יהוה
אֱלֹהֵינוּ מֶלֶךְ הָעוֹלָם,
אֲשֶׁר בָּרָא שָׂשׂוֹן וְשִׂמְחָה,
חָתָן וְכַלָּה,
גִּילָה, רִנָּה, דִּיצָה וְחֶדְוָה,
אַהֲבָה וְאַחֲוָה
וְשָׁלוֹם וְרֵעוּת.
מְהֵרָה, יהוה אֱלֹהֵינוּ,
יִשָּׁמַע בְּעָרֵי יְהוּדָה
וּבְחוּצוֹת יְרוּשָׁלַיִם

Blessed art Thou, O Lord our God, King of the universe, Who created joy and gladness, bridegroom and bride, mirth, song, dancing and jubilation, love and harmony, peace and fellowship. O Lord our God, may there soon be heard in the cities of Judah and the streets of Jerusalem

קוֹל שָׂשׂוֹן וְקוֹל שִׂמְחָה,
קוֹל חָתָן וְקוֹל כַּלָּה,
קוֹל מִצְהֲלוֹת
חֲתָנִים מֵחֻפָּתָם
וּנְעָרִים מִמִּשְׁתֵּה נְגִינָתָם.
בָּרוּךְ אַתָּה יהוה
מְשַׂמֵּחַ חָתָן עִם הַכַּלָּה.

the sound of joy and the sound of gladness, the voice of the bridegroom and the voice of the bride, the jubilant voices of bridegrooms from their canopies and of youths from their feasts of song. Blessed art Thou, O Lord, Who causes the bridegroom to rejoice with the bride.

After the ceremony the bridegroom and bride go into a room and remain there alone for a short while. Two witnesses wait outside.

The Ketubah

The *ketubah* is a document in which a husband's duties to his wife are set forth. It is written in Aramaic, the vernacular of the Talmudic period. Here is a translation:

On the ... day of the week, on the ... day of the month of ... in the year ... from the creation of the world according to the era which we are counting, here in the city of ...

(Groom's name) said unto the virgin (bride's name) "Be Thou my wife according to the law of Moses and of Israel. I will work for thee, honour, maintain and provide for thee in accordance with the custom of Jewish husbands who work for their wives, and honour, maintain and provide for

them, and I give thee two hundred zuzim, the mohar (bride-price) in lieu of thy virginity, which are due to thee according to the Torah, and thy food and clothing and all thy need, and I will live with thee in conjugal relations according to the way of all the world."

And the bride, the virgin (bride's name) consented to become his wife. And this is the dowry she brought from her father's house: silver, gold, jewels and clothes to the value of ..., and the bridegroom consented to add to this amount...

Then said the bridegroom ... : "It shall be my responsibility and the responsibility of my heirs after me to see to it that the undertakings of this ketubah and the additions to the ketubah are paid from the property I have acquired or shall acquire in the future, with or without obligations. All these shall be pledged to pay out this ketubah and the additions thereto, even the mantle on my shoulders, both while I am alive and after my death, even from this day and for evermore."

And the bridegroom (name) has taken upon himself the responsibilities of this ketubah and these additions, according to the stringent interpretation of all the ketubot and additions that are customary to be drawn up in favour of the daughters of Israel by our Sages of blessed memory. It is not to be treated as an illusory obligation or as merely a formal draft.

And we have obtained from (groom's name) bridegroom of (bride's name) consent for everything that is written and explained heretofore, through the legal formality of kinyan, by means of an instrument legally fit for the purpose, and all is now valid and established.

Signatures of the bridegroom and two witnesses.

וְאָכַלְתָּ וְשָׂבָעְתָּ
וּבֵרַכְתָּ אֶת־יהוה אֱלֹהֶיךָ
עַל־הָאָרֶץ הַטֹּבָה
אֲשֶׁר נָתַן־לָךְ׃

Grace After Meals

"And thou shalt eat and be satisfied, and bless the Lord thy God for the good land which He hath given thee." (Deuteronomy 8:10)

We are commanded in the Bible to say the Grace After Meals, and the Talmudic Sages decreed that it should be said after every meal that includes bread. The Grace After Meals consists of four blessings — the blessing of the "Provider," which according to the Talmud was composed by Moses when the manna was given in the desert; the "blessing on the Land," said to have been composed by Joshua after he led the Israelites into the Land of Israel; the "Jerusalem" blessing ascribed to David and Solomon; and the "Who is good and doeth good" blessing composed at Yavneh on the day when the slain of Betar were buried. The Great Assembly decided on the basic form of the Grace — as of most of the Jewish prayers and blessings — and a few slight additions were made in the Tannaic period and later. Special additions were also made for Sabbaths and festivals and various ceremonial meals.

On the Sabbath, on festivals and at ceremonial meals the following Psalm is said before Grace:

שִׁיר הַמַּעֲלוֹת, בְּשׁוּב יהוה אֶת שִׁיבַת צִיּוֹן הָיִינוּ כְּחֹלְמִים: אָז יִמָּלֵא שְׂחוֹק פִּינוּ וּלְשׁוֹנֵנוּ רִנָּה, אָז יֹאמְרוּ בַגּוֹיִם הִגְדִּיל יהוה לַעֲשׂוֹת עִם אֵלֶּה: הִגְדִּיל יהוה לַעֲשׂוֹת עִמָּנוּ, הָיִינוּ שְׂמֵחִים: שׁוּבָה יהוה אֶת שְׁבִיתֵנוּ כַּאֲפִיקִים בַּנֶּגֶב: הַזֹּרְעִים בְּדִמְעָה בְּרִנָּה יִקְצֹרוּ. הָלוֹךְ יֵלֵךְ וּבָכֹה נֹשֵׂא מֶשֶׁךְ הַזָּרַע, בֹּא יָבֹא בְרִנָּה, נֹשֵׂא אֲלֻמֹּתָיו:

A psalm of degrees.
When the Lord turned again the captivity of Zion, we were like them that dream.
Then was our mouth filled with laughter, and our tongue with singing: then said they among the heathen: "The Lord hath done great things for them."
The Lord hath done great things for us, whereof we are glad.
Turn again our captivity, O Lord, as the streams in the south.
They that sow in tears shall reap in joy.
He that goeth forth and weepeth, bearing his seed bag, shall doubtless come again with rejoicing, bringing his sheaves with him. *(Psalm 126)*

A recurrent idea in Judaism is that we cannot assume that anything in the world is ours by right, and so a man is forbidden to enjoy anything in the world without blessing God for it.

The Grace

When three or more men have eaten together, one of them begins:

רַבּוֹתַי, נְבָרֵךְ.   Gentlemen, let us say Grace.

The others respond:

יְהִי שֵׁם יהוה מְבֹרָךְ מֵעַתָּה וְעַד עוֹלָם.

Blessed be the name of the Lord for ever and ever.

He repeats:

יְהִי שֵׁם יהוה מְבֹרָךְ מֵעַתָּה וְעַד עוֹלָם.

Blessed be the name of the Lord for ever and ever.

At a wedding-feast he says:

דְּוַי הָסֵר וְגַם חָרוֹן, וְאָז אִלֵּם בְּשִׁיר יָרֹן.
נְחֵנוּ בְּמַעְגְּלֵי צֶדֶק, שְׁעֵה בִּרְכַּת בְּנֵי אַהֲרֹן.

O banish grief and wrath, and let the speechless break forth into song. Guide us in the paths of righteousness; heed the blessing of the sons of Aaron (the Cohanim).

At a circumcision feast he says:

נוֹדֶה לְשִׁמְךָ בְּתוֹךְ אֱמוּנַי,
בְּרוּכִים אַתֶּם לַיהוה.

We praise Thy name among the faithful:
May you be blessed by the Lord.

בִּרְשׁוּת אֵל אָיוֹם וְנוֹרָא,
מִשְׂגָּב לְעִתּוֹת בַּצָּרָה,
אֵל נֶאְזָר בִּגְבוּרָה,
אַדִּיר בַּמָּרוֹם יהוה.

By permission of the awesome and revered God,
A refuge in time of distress,
The God girt with strength,
Mighty on high, the Lord.

בִּרְשׁוּת הַתּוֹרָה הַקְּדוֹשָׁה,
טְהוֹרָה הִיא וְגַם פְּרוּשָׁה,
צִוָּה לָנוּ מוֹרָשָׁה,
מֹשֶׁה עֶבֶד יהוה.

By permission of the holy Torah,
Pure and clear,
Bequeathed to us as an inheritance
By Moses, servant of the Lord.

בִּרְשׁוּת הַכֹּהֲנִים וְהַלְוִיִּם,
אֶקְרָא לֵאלֹהֵי הָעִבְרִיִּים,
אֲהוֹדֶנּוּ בְּכָל אִיִּים,
אֲבָרְכָה אֶת יהוה.

By permission of the Cohanim and Levites
I will call upon the God of the Hebrews,
And singing His praises in every region
I will bless the Lord.

בִּרְשׁוּת מָרָנָן וְרַבָּנָן וְרַבּוֹתַי
אֶפְתְּחָה בְּשִׁיר פִּי וּשְׂפָתַי,
וְתֹאמַרְנָה עַצְמוֹתַי,
בָּרוּךְ הַבָּא בְּשֵׁם יהוה.

By permission of all those gathered here
I will open my mouth and lips in song,
And my entire body shall proclaim:
"Blessed is he that cometh in the name of the Lord."

48

בִּרְשׁוּת רַבּוֹתַי, נְבָרֵךְ (בעשרה אנשים מוסיף: אֱלֹהֵינוּ, ובסעודת שמחה מוסיף: שֶׁהַשִּׂמְחָה בִּמְעוֹנוֹ) שֶׁאָכַלְנוּ מִשֶּׁלּוֹ.

Gentlemen, by your leave, let us bless Him (when ten men are present, add: our God; at a festive meal, such as at a wedding and a circumcision ceremony, add: in Whose abode the celebration is taking place) Whose food we have eaten.

The others respond:

בָּרוּךְ (אֱלֹהֵינוּ, שֶׁהַשִּׂמְחָה בִּמְעוֹנוֹ) שֶׁאָכַלְנוּ מִשֶּׁלּוֹ וּבְטוּבוֹ חָיִינוּ.

Blessed be He (our God, in Whose abode the celebration is taking place) Whose food we have eaten and by Whose goodness we live.

He repeats:

בָּרוּךְ (אֱלֹהֵינוּ, שֶׁהַשִּׂמְחָה בִּמְעוֹנוֹ) שֶׁאָכַלְנוּ מִשֶּׁלּוֹ וּבְטוּבוֹ חָיִינוּ.

Blessed be He (our God, in Whose abode the celebration is taking place) Whose food we have eaten and by Whose goodness we live.

(The blessing of the "Provider")

בָּרוּךְ אַתָּה יהוה אֱלֹהֵינוּ מֶלֶךְ הָעוֹלָם, הַזָּן אֶת הָעוֹלָם כֻּלּוֹ בְּטוּבוֹ, בְּחֵן וּבְחֶסֶד וּבְרַחֲמִים, הוּא נוֹתֵן לֶחֶם לְכָל בָּשָׂר, כִּי לְעוֹלָם חַסְדּוֹ. וּבְטוּבוֹ הַגָּדוֹל תָּמִיד לֹא חָסַר-לָנוּ וְאַל יֶחְסַר לָנוּ מָזוֹן לְעוֹלָם וָעֶד, בַּעֲבוּר שְׁמוֹ הַגָּדוֹל, כִּי הוּא אֵל זָן וּמְפַרְנֵס לַכֹּל וּמֵטִיב לַכֹּל וּמֵכִין מָזוֹן לְכָל בְּרִיּוֹתָיו אֲשֶׁר בָּרָא. בָּרוּךְ אַתָּה יהוה, הַזָּן אֶת הַכֹּל.

Blessed art Thou, O Lord our God, King of the universe, Who feeds the whole world in His goodness, and with grace, mercy and compassion. "He giveth food to every creature, for His mercy endureth for ever" (Psalm 136:25). And through His abundant goodness, we have never been in want, and may we never be in want of sustenance, for His great name's sake, for He feeds and sustains all, is good to all, and provides food for all the creatures He has created. Blessed art Thou, O Lord, Who feeds all.

(The blessing on the Land)

נוֹדֶה לְךָ, יהוה אֱלֹהֵינוּ, עַל
שֶׁהִנְחַלְתָּ לַאֲבוֹתֵינוּ אֶרֶץ
חֶמְדָּה טוֹבָה וּרְחָבָה, וְעַל
שֶׁהוֹצֵאתָנוּ יהוה אֱלֹהֵינוּ
מֵאֶרֶץ מִצְרַיִם, וּפְדִיתָנוּ מִבֵּית
עֲבָדִים, וְעַל בְּרִיתְךָ שֶׁחָתַמְתָּ
בִּבְשָׂרֵנוּ, וְעַל תּוֹרָתְךָ
שֶׁלִּמַּדְתָּנוּ, וְעַל חֻקֶּיךָ
שֶׁהוֹדַעְתָּנוּ, וְעַל חַיִּים חֵן וָחֶסֶד
שֶׁחוֹנַנְתָּנוּ, וְעַל אֲכִילַת מָזוֹן
שָׁאַתָּה זָן וּמְפַרְנֵס אוֹתָנוּ
תָּמִיד, בְּכָל יוֹם וּבְכָל עֵת וּבְכָל
שָׁעָה.

We thank Thee, O Lord our God, for the
bequeathing to our fathers a lovely, goodly
and spacious land, and for bringing us, O
Lord our God, out of the land of Egypt and
redeeming us from the house of bondage,
for the Covenant that Thou hast sealed in
our flesh, for Thy Torah that Thou hast
taught us, and for Thy statutes that Thou
hast made known to us; for the life, grace,
and mercy with which Thou hast favoured
us, and for the food that Thou dost grant
us constantly, every day, at every time and
at every hour.

On *Hanukkah* and *Purim* say:

עַל הַנִּסִּים וְעַל הַפֻּרְקָן וְעַל הַגְּבוּרוֹת וְעַל הַתְּשׁוּעוֹת וְעַל הַמִּלְחָמוֹת שֶׁעָשִׂיתָ לַאֲבוֹתֵינוּ בַּיָּמִים הָהֵם בַּזְּמַן הַזֶּה.

And for the miracles, and for the redemption, and for the mighty deeds, and for the triumphs, and for the wonders, and for the consolations, and for the wars which Thou didst perform for our fathers in those days at this season.

On *Hanukkah* say:

בִּימֵי מַתִּתְיָהוּ בֶּן יוֹחָנָן כֹּהֵן גָּדוֹל חַשְׁמוֹנַאי וּבָנָיו, כְּשֶׁעָמְדָה מַלְכוּת יָוָן הָרְשָׁעָה עַל עַמְּךָ יִשְׂרָאֵל, לְהַשְׁכִּיחָם תּוֹרָתֶךָ וּלְהַעֲבִירָם מֵחֻקֵּי רְצוֹנֶךָ, וְאַתָּה בְּרַחֲמֶיךָ הָרַבִּים, עָמַדְתָּ לָהֶם בְּעֵת צָרָתָם, רַבְתָּ אֶת רִיבָם, דַּנְתָּ אֶת דִּינָם, נָקַמְתָּ אֶת נִקְמָתָם, מָסַרְתָּ גִבּוֹרִים בְּיַד חַלָּשִׁים, וְרַבִּים בְּיַד מְעַטִּים, וּטְמֵאִים בְּיַד טְהוֹרִים, וּרְשָׁעִים בְּיַד צַדִּיקִים, וְזֵדִים בְּיַד עוֹסְקֵי תוֹרָתֶךָ. וּלְךָ עָשִׂיתָ שֵׁם גָּדוֹל וְקָדוֹשׁ בְּעוֹלָמֶךָ, וּלְעַמְּךָ יִשְׂרָאֵל עָשִׂיתָ תְּשׁוּעָה גְדוֹלָה וּפֻרְקָן כְּהַיּוֹם הַזֶּה. וְאַחַר כֵּן בָּאוּ בָנֶיךָ לִדְבִיר בֵּיתֶךָ, וּפִנּוּ אֶת הֵיכָלֶךָ, וְטִהֲרוּ אֶת מִקְדָּשֶׁךָ, וְהִדְלִיקוּ נֵרוֹת בְּחַצְרוֹת קָדְשֶׁךָ, וְקָבְעוּ שְׁמוֹנַת יְמֵי חֲנֻכָּה אֵלוּ, לְהוֹדוֹת וּלְהַלֵּל לְשִׁמְךָ הַגָּדוֹל.

In the days of Hasmonean Mattathias ben Yohanan the High Priest and his sons, when the wicked Hellenic government arose against Thy people Israel to compel them to forsake Thy Torah and transgress the commandments of Thy will, Thou in Thy great mercy didst stand by them in their distress. Thou didst champion their cause; Thou didst defend their rights; Thou didst avenge their wrong; Thou didst deliver the strong into the hands of the weak, the many into the hands of the few, the impure into the hands of the pure, the wicked into the hands of the upright, and the evil into the hands of those who occupied themselves with Thy Torah. For Thyself Thou didst make a great and holy name in Thy work, and for Israel Thy people didst Thou work a mighty deliverance and redemption, as at this day. And then Thy children entered the shrine of Thy house, cleansed Thy Temple, purified Thy sanctuary, kindled lights in Thy holy courts and established these eight days of *Hanukkah* for giving thanks and praise to Thy great name.

At *Purim* say:

בִּימֵי מָרְדְּכַי וְאֶסְתֵּר בְּשׁוּשַׁן הַבִּירָה, כְּשֶׁעָמַד עֲלֵיהֶם הָמָן הָרָשָׁע, בִּקֵּשׁ לְהַשְׁמִיד לַהֲרֹג וּלְאַבֵּד אֶת כָּל הַיְּהוּדִים, מִנַּעַר וְעַד זָקֵן, טַף וְנָשִׁים, בְּיוֹם אֶחָד, בִּשְׁלֹשָׁה עָשָׂר לְחֹדֶשׁ שְׁנֵים עָשָׂר, הוּא חֹדֶשׁ אֲדָר וּשְׁלָלָם לָבוֹז. וְאַתָּה

In the days of Mordecai and Esther, in Shushan the capital, when the wicked Haman rose up against them, and sought to annihilate, to slay and destroy all the Jews, young and old, infants and women, in one day, on the thirteenth day of the twelfth month, Adar, and their possessions open to plunder, then didst Thou in Thy

בְּרַחֲמֶיךָ הָרַבִּים הָפַרְתָּ אֶת עֲצָתוֹ, וְקִלְקַלְתָּ אֶת
מַחֲשַׁבְתּוֹ, וַהֲשֵׁבוֹתָ לוֹ גְמוּלוֹ בְּרֹאשׁוֹ, וְתָלוּ
אוֹתוֹ וְאֶת בָּנָיו עַל הָעֵץ.

great mercy frustrate his design, undo his plot and cause his scheme to rebound on him; and him and his sons they hanged on the gallows.

וְעַל הַכֹּל יהוה אֱלֹהֵינוּ אֲנַחְנוּ
מוֹדִים לָךְ וּמְבָרְכִים אוֹתָךְ,
יִתְבָּרַךְ שִׁמְךָ בְּפִי כָל חַי תָּמִיד
לְעוֹלָם וָעֶד, כַּכָּתוּב: וְאָכַלְתָּ
וְשָׂבָעְתָּ וּבֵרַכְתָּ אֶת יהוה
אֱלֹהֶיךָ עַל הָאָרֶץ הַטֹּבָה אֲשֶׁר
נָתַן לָךְ: בָּרוּךְ אַתָּה יהוה, עַל
הָאָרֶץ וְעַל הַמָּזוֹן.

And for all this, O Lord our God, we thank and bless Thee, blessed by Thy name in the mouth of all that lives, continually for evermore. As it is written: "When thou hast eaten and art satisfied, then shalt thou bless the Lord thy God, for the goodly land that He gave thee" *(Deuteronomy 8:10).* Blessed art Thou, O Lord, for the land and for the sustenance.

(The "Jerusalem" blessing)

רַחֶם־נָא יהוה אֱלֹהֵינוּ עַל
יִשְׂרָאֵל עַמֶּךָ, וְעַל יְרוּשָׁלַיִם
עִירֶךָ וְעַל צִיּוֹן מִשְׁכַּן כְּבוֹדֶךָ
וְעַל מַלְכוּת בֵּית דָּוִד מְשִׁיחֶךָ
וְעַל הַבַּיִת הַגָּדוֹל וְהַקָּדוֹשׁ
שֶׁנִּקְרָא שִׁמְךָ עָלָיו. אֱלֹהֵינוּ,
אָבִינוּ, רְעֵנוּ זוּנֵנוּ פַּרְנְסֵנוּ
וְכַלְכְּלֵנוּ וְהַרְוִיחֵנוּ, וְהַרְוַח לָנוּ
יהוה אֱלֹהֵינוּ מְהֵרָה מִכָּל

Have mercy, O Lord our God, on Thy people Israel, on Jerusalem Thy city, on Zion the abode of Thy glory, on the kingdom of the house of David Thy anointed and on the great and holy House that bears Thy name. Our God, our father, shepherd us, nourish us, sustain us and maintain us, and cause us to prosper, and speedily, O Lord our God, deliver us from

צָרוֹתֵינוּ, וְנָא אַל תַּצְרִיכֵנוּ
יהוה אֱלֹהֵינוּ לֹא לִידֵי מַתְּנַת
בָּשָׂר וָדָם וְלֹא לִידֵי הַלְוָאָתָם,
כִּי אִם לְיָדְךָ הַמְּלֵאָה, הַפְּתוּחָה,
הַקְּדוֹשָׁה וְהָרְחָבָה, שֶׁלֹּא נֵבוֹשׁ
וְלֹא נִכָּלֵם לְעוֹלָם וָעֶד.

all our troubles. And please, O Lord our God, cause us never to be in need of gifts of men, or of their loans, but only of Thy full, open, holy and generous hand, that we may never be ashamed or disgraced, or stumble, ever.

"The fastidious people of Jerusalem never sat down to a feast without first ascertaining who would be sitting with them."

On the Sabbath say:

רְצֵה וְהַחֲלִיצֵנוּ יהוה אֱלֹהֵינוּ בְּמִצְוֹתֶיךָ
וּבְמִצְוַת יוֹם הַשְּׁבִיעִי הַשַּׁבָּת הַגָּדוֹל וְהַקָּדוֹשׁ
הַזֶּה, כִּי יוֹם זֶה גָּדוֹל וְקָדוֹשׁ הוּא לְפָנֶיךָ
לִשְׁבָּת־בּוֹ וְלָנוּחַ בּוֹ בְּאַהֲבָה כְּמִצְוַת רְצוֹנֶךָ,
וּבִרְצוֹנְךָ הָנִיחַ לָנוּ, יהוה אֱלֹהֵינוּ, שֶׁלֹּא תְהֵא
צָרָה וְיָגוֹן וַאֲנָחָה בְּיוֹם מְנוּחָתֵנוּ, וְהַרְאֵנוּ יהוה
אֱלֹהֵינוּ בְּנֶחָמַת צִיּוֹן עִירֶךָ וּבְבִנְיַן יְרוּשָׁלַיִם עִיר
קָדְשֶׁךָ, כִּי אַתָּה הוּא בַּעַל הַיְשׁוּעוֹת וּבַעַל
הַנֶּחָמוֹת.

Be pleased, O Lord our God, to strengthen us with Thy commandments, and with the commandment concerning the seventh day, this great and holy Sabbath. For this is a great and holy day to Thee, to abstain from work and rest, according to Thy will. And may it be Thy will, O Lord our God, that there be no trouble, worry, anguish or affliction on our day of rest, and show us, O Lord our God, the consolation of Zion Thy city and the building of Jerusalem Thy holy city, for Thou art the master of all salvation and the master of all consolation.

On *Rosh Hodesh*, festivals, and *Rosh Hashanah* say:

אֱלֹהֵינוּ וֵאלֹהֵי אֲבוֹתֵינוּ יַעֲלֶה וְיָבֹא וְיַגִּיעַ,
וְיֵרָאֶה וְיֵרָצֶה וְיִשָּׁמַע, וְיִפָּקֵד וְיִזָּכֵר זִכְרוֹנֵנוּ
וּפִקְדוֹנֵנוּ וְזִכְרוֹן אֲבוֹתֵינוּ, וְזִכְרוֹן מָשִׁיחַ בֶּן דָּוִד

Our God and God of our fathers, may there rise, and come and arrive, and be seen and accepted and heard, and be visited and remembered, our remembrance and the remembrance of our fathers, the remembrance of the Messiah, son of David Thy

עַבְדֶּךָ, וְזִכְרוֹן יְרוּשָׁלַיִם עִיר קָדְשֶׁךָ, וְזִכְרוֹן כָּל עַמְּךָ בֵּית יִשְׂרָאֵל, לְפָנֶיךָ, לִפְלֵיטָה לְטוֹבָה, לְחֵן וּלְחֶסֶד וּלְרַחֲמִים, לְחַיִּים וּלְשָׁלוֹם בְּיוֹם

servant, the remembrance of Jerusalem Thy holy city and the remembrance of all Thy people, the house of Israel: for deliverance, for good and for grace, for kindness, for mercy, for life and for peace on this day.

בראש חודש: רֹאשׁ הַחֹדֶשׁ הַזֶּה.

On *Rosh Hodesh* (the New Moon) say — of *Rosh Hodesh*.

בפסח: חַג הַמַּצּוֹת הַזֶּה.

On *Pessach* (Passover) say — the feast of *matzot*.

בשבועות: חַג הַשָּׁבוּעוֹת הַזֶּה.

On *Shavuot* (the Feast of Weeks) say — the feast of *Shavuot*.

בסוכות: חַג הַסֻּכּוֹת הַזֶּה.

On *Succot* (the Feast of Tabernacles) say — the feast of *Succot*.

בשמיני עצרת: הַשְּׁמִינִי חַג הָעֲצֶרֶת הַזֶּה.

On *Shemini Atseret* (the Eighth Day of Assembly) say — *Shemini Atseret*.

בראש השנה: הַזִּכָּרוֹן הַזֶּה.

On *Rosh Hashana* (the New Year) say — of Remembrance.

לילדים האוכלים ביום כפור: הַכִּפּוּרִים הַזֶּה.

Children eating on *Yom Kippur* (the Day of Atonement) say — of Atonement.

זָכְרֵנוּ יהוה אֱלֹהֵינוּ בּוֹ לְטוֹבָה, וּפָקְדֵנוּ בוֹ לִבְרָכָה, וְהוֹשִׁיעֵנוּ בוֹ לְחַיִּים. וּבִדְבַר יְשׁוּעָה וְרַחֲמִים חוּס וְחָנֵּנוּ וְרַחֵם עָלֵינוּ וְהוֹשִׁיעֵנוּ, כִּי אֵלֶיךָ עֵינֵינוּ, כִּי אֵל מֶלֶךְ חַנּוּן וְרַחוּם אָתָּה.

On this day remember us, O Lord our God, for good, and visit us for a blessing, and save us for a good life. And with words of salvation and mercy, pity us and be gracious to us, be merciful to us and redeem us, for our eyes look always to Thee, for Thou art a gracious and merciful king.

וּבְנֵה יְרוּשָׁלַיִם עִיר הַקֹּדֶשׁ בִּמְהֵרָה בְיָמֵינוּ. בָּרוּךְ אַתָּה יהוה, בּוֹנֵה בְרַחֲמָיו יְרוּשָׁלָיִם. אָמֵן.

And rebuild Jerusalem, the holy city, soon, in our days.
Blessed art Thou, O Lord, Who in His mercy builds Jerusalem, Amen.

(The "Who is good and doeth good" blessing)

בָּרוּךְ אַתָּה יהוה אֱלֹהֵינוּ מֶלֶךְ

Blessed art Thou, O Lord our God, King of the

הָעוֹלָם, הָאֵל, אָבִינוּ, מַלְכֵּנוּ, אַדִּירֵנוּ, בּוֹרְאֵנוּ, גּוֹאֲלֵנוּ, יוֹצְרֵנוּ, קְדוֹשֵׁנוּ קְדוֹשׁ יַעֲקֹב, רוֹעֵנוּ רוֹעֵה יִשְׂרָאֵל, הַמֶּלֶךְ הַטּוֹב וְהַמֵּטִיב לַכֹּל, שֶׁבְּכָל יוֹם וָיוֹם הוּא הֵיטִיב הוּא מֵיטִיב הוּא יֵיטִיב לָנוּ, הוּא גְמָלָנוּ הוּא גוֹמְלֵנוּ הוּא יִגְמְלֵנוּ לָעַד לְחֵן וּלְחֶסֶד וּלְרַחֲמִים וּלְרֶוַח, הַצָּלָה וְהַצְלָחָה, בְּרָכָה וִישׁוּעָה, נֶחָמָה, פַּרְנָסָה וְכַלְכָּלָה, וְרַחֲמִים וְחַיִּים וְשָׁלוֹם וְכָל טוֹב, וּמִכָּל טוּב לְעוֹלָם אַל יְחַסְּרֵנוּ.

הָרַחֲמָן הוּא יִמְלֹךְ עָלֵינוּ לְעוֹלָם וָעֶד. הָרַחֲמָן הוּא יִתְבָּרַךְ בַּשָּׁמַיִם וּבָאָרֶץ. הָרַחֲמָן הוּא יִשְׁתַּבַּח לְדוֹר דּוֹרִים, וְיִתְפָּאַר בָּנוּ לָעַד וּלְנֵצַח נְצָחִים, וְיִתְהַדַּר בָּנוּ לָעַד וּלְעוֹלְמֵי עוֹלָמִים. הָרַחֲמָן הוּא יְפַרְנְסֵנוּ בְּכָבוֹד. הָרַחֲמָן הוּא

universe. O God, our father, our king, our mighty one, our creator, our redeemer, our maker, our Holy One, the Holy One of Jacob; our shepherd, the shepherd of Israel; the good king Who is good to all, and each and every day did, does and will deal kindly with us always, for grace, favour, mercy and deliverance; freedom, protection, prosperity, blessing, salvation, comfort, support, sustenance, mercy, life, peace, and all good; and may we never lack for any good thing.

May the All-Merciful reign over us for ever and ever.
May the All-Merciful be blessed in heaven and on earth.
May the All-Merciful be praised throughout all generations; may He be glorified in us for all ages and honoured in us now and for all eternity.
May the All-Merciful sustain us respectably.

יִשְׁבֹּר עֻלֵּנוּ מֵעַל צַוָּארֵנוּ וְהוּא
יוֹלִיכֵנוּ קוֹמְמִיּוּת לְאַרְצֵנוּ.
הָרַחֲמָן הוּא יִשְׁלַח לָנוּ בְּרָכָה
מְרֻבָּה בַּבַּיִת הַזֶּה וְעַל שֻׁלְחָן זֶה
שֶׁאָכַלְנוּ עָלָיו. הָרַחֲמָן הוּא
יִשְׁלַח לָנוּ אֶת אֵלִיָּהוּ הַנָּבִיא
זָכוּר לַטּוֹב וִיבַשֶּׂר־לָנוּ בְּשׂוֹרוֹת
טוֹבוֹת יְשׁוּעוֹת וְנֶחָמוֹת.
הָרַחֲמָן הוּא יְבָרֵךְ אֶת אָבִי
מוֹרִי בַּעַל הַבַּיִת הַזֶּה וְאֶת אִמִּי
מוֹרָתִי בַּעֲלַת הַבַּיִת הַזֶּה, אוֹתָם
וְאֶת בֵּיתָם וְאֶת זַרְעָם וְאֶת כָּל
אֲשֶׁר לָהֶם. (אוֹתִי וְאֶת אִשְׁתִּי
וְאֶת זַרְעִי וְאֶת כָּל אֲשֶׁר לִי),
אוֹתָנוּ וְאֶת כָּל אֲשֶׁר לָנוּ, כְּמוֹ
שֶׁנִּתְבָּרְכוּ אֲבוֹתֵינוּ אַבְרָהָם
יִצְחָק וְיַעֲקֹב בַּכֹּל מִכֹּל כֹּל, כֵּן
יְבָרֵךְ אוֹתָנוּ כֻּלָּנוּ יַחַד בִּבְרָכָה
שְׁלֵמָה, וְנֹאמַר אָמֵן.

בַּמָּרוֹם יְלַמְּדוּ עֲלֵיהֶם וְעָלֵינוּ
זְכוּת שֶׁתְּהֵא לְמִשְׁמֶרֶת שָׁלוֹם,

May the All-Merciful break the yoke from our neck and lead us upright into our land.
May the All-Merciful multiply blessings on this house, and on this table at which we have eaten.
May the All-Merciful send us the Prophet Elijah of blessed memory to bring us good tidings of deliverance and comfort.

One eating at one's own table says (omitting whichever of the bracketed items is inappropriate):

May the All-Merciful bless me (and my father and mother) (and my wife and offspring) (and my husband and offspring) (and all the others seated here),

A guest says:

May the All-Merciful bless (my revered father), (the master of this house) and (my revered mother), (the mistress of this house), them and their household and their offspring and all that is theirs; us, and all that belongs to us. As our fathers Abraham, Issac and Jacob were blessed with all and every good, so may He bless us all together with complete blessing. And let us say, Amen.

May their merits and may ours, made known On High, be a store of peace treasured up for

וְנִשָּׂא בְרָכָה מֵאֵת יהוה,
וּצְדָקָה מֵאֱלֹהֵי יִשְׁעֵנוּ, וְנִמְצָא
חֵן וְשֵׂכֶל טוֹב בְּעֵינֵי אֱלֹהִים
וְאָדָם.

us. And may we receive a blessing from the Lord and righteousness from the God of our salvation. And may we find grace and favour in the eyes of God and people.

> *A Jew is required to perform even the simplest of banal acts with sanctity. Thus, the table at which we eat is compared to an altar, and this concept determines our behaviour while eating.*

At a circumcision feast say (the listeners answering Amen after each stanza):

הָרַחֲמָן הוּא יְבָרֵךְ אֲבִי הַיֶּלֶד וְאִמּוֹ, וְיִזְכּוּ לְגַדְּלוֹ
וּלְחַנְּכוֹ וּלְחַכְּמוֹ, מִיּוֹם הַשְּׁמִינִי וָהָלְאָה יֵרָצֶה
דָּמוֹ, וִיהִי יהוה אֱלֹהָיו עִמּוֹ.

May the All-Merciful bless the father and mother of this child; may they have the privilege of rearing him and educating him and teaching him wisdom. From this eighth day onward may his blood find acceptance, and may the Lord his God be with him.

הָרַחֲמָן הוּא יְבָרֵךְ בַּעַל בְּרִית הַמִּילָה, אֲשֶׁר
שָׂשׂ לַעֲשׂוֹת צֶדֶק בְּגִילָה, וִישַׁלֵּם פָּעֳלוֹ
וּמַשְׂכֻּרְתּוֹ כְּפוּלָה, וְיִתְּנֵהוּ לְמַעְלָה לְמָעְלָה.

May the All-Merciful bless the master of this festivity, who has rejoiced to do this righteous act, and may God recompense him doubly and raise him up on high.

הָרַחֲמָן הוּא יְבָרֵךְ רַךְ הַנִּמּוֹל לִשְׁמוֹנָה, וְיִהְיוּ
יָדָיו וְלִבּוֹ לָאֵל אֱמוּנָה, וְיִזְכֶּה לִרְאוֹת פְּנֵי
הַשְּׁכִינָה, שָׁלֹשׁ פְּעָמִים בַּשָּׁנָה.

May the All-Merciful bless this tender babe just circumcised. May his hands and heart be true to God, and may he be privileged to appear before the Divine Presence three times a year.

הָרַחֲמָן הוּא יְבָרֵךְ הַמָּל בְּשַׂר הָעָרְלָה, וּפָרַע
וּמָצַץ דְּמֵי הַמִּילָה, אִישׁ הַיָּרֵא וְרַךְ הַלֵּבָב
עֲבוֹדָתוֹ פְּסוּלָה, אִם שְׁלָשׁ אֵלֶּה לֹא יַעֲשֶׂה לָהּ.

May the All-Merciful bless him who removed the foreskin, and sucked the blood of the circumcision. Were he timid or fainthearted, or did he fail to fulfil the essentials of the rite, his work would have been invalid.

הָרַחֲמָן הוּא יִשְׁלַח לָנוּ מְשִׁיחוֹ הוֹלֵךְ תָּמִים, בִּזְכוּת חֲתַן לַמּוּלוֹת דָּמִים, לְבַשֵּׂר בְּשׂוֹרוֹת טוֹבוֹת וְנִחוּמִים, לְעַם אֶחָד מְפֻזָּר וּמְפֹרָד בֵּין הָעַמִּים.

May the All-Merciful, for the sake of our innocent children, send us the blameless anointed one (Elijah), to bring good tidings and consolation to a people scattered and dispersed among the nations.

הָרַחֲמָן הוּא יִשְׁלַח לָנוּ כֹּהֵן צֶדֶק אֲשֶׁר לֻקַּח לְעֵילָם, עַד הוּכַן כִּסְאוֹ כַּשֶּׁמֶשׁ וְיַהֲלֹם, וַיָּלֶט פָּנָיו בְּאַדַּרְתּוֹ וַיִּגְלֹם, בְּרִיתִי הָיְתָה אִתּוֹ הַחַיִּים וְהַשָּׁלוֹם.

May the All-Merciful send us the righteous priest (Elijah) who remains withdrawn until a throne, bright as the sun and as the diamond, is prepared for him who hid his face in his mantle and with whom is God's covenant of love and peace.

On the Sabbath say:

בשבת: הָרַחֲמָן הוּא יַנְחִילֵנוּ יוֹם שֶׁכֻּלּוֹ שַׁבָּת וּמְנוּחָה לְחַיֵּי הָעוֹלָמִים.

May the All-Merciful grant us the day that is entirely Sabbath and rest for life everlasting.

On *Rosh Hodesh* say:

בראש חודש: הָרַחֲמָן הוּא יְחַדֵּשׁ עָלֵינוּ אֶת הַחֹדֶשׁ הַזֶּה לְטוֹבָה וְלִבְרָכָה.

May the All-Merciful cause this new month to be one of happiness and blessing for us.

On a festival say:

ביום טוב: הָרַחֲמָן הוּא יַנְחִילֵנוּ יוֹם שֶׁכֻּלּוֹ טוֹב.

May the All-Merciful grant us a day that is entirely good.

On *Rosh Hashana* say:

בראש השנה: הָרַחֲמָן הוּא יְחַדֵּשׁ עָלֵינוּ אֶת הַשָּׁנָה הַזֹּאת לְטוֹבָה וְלִבְרָכָה.

May the All-Merciful cause this new year to be one of happiness and blessing for us.

On *Succot* say:

בסוכות: הָרַחֲמָן הוּא יָקִים לָנוּ אֶת סֻכַּת דָּוִד הַנּוֹפֶלֶת.

May the All-Merciful restore to us the fallen tabernacle of David.

הָרַחֲמָן הוּא יְזַכֵּנוּ לִימוֹת הַמָּשִׁיחַ וּלְחַיֵּי הָעוֹלָם הַבָּא.

May the All-Merciful make us worthy of the days of the Messiah and of the life of the World-to-Come. "He is a tower of salvation

58

מַגְדִּיל (בשבת וביום טוב וחול המועד וראש חודש :

מִגְדּוֹל) יְשׁוּעוֹת מַלְכּוֹ וְעֹשֶׂה
חֶסֶד לִמְשִׁיחוֹ, לְדָוִד וּלְזַרְעוֹ עַד
עוֹלָם : עֹשֶׂה שָׁלוֹם בִּמְרוֹמָיו
הוּא יַעֲשֶׂה שָׁלוֹם עָלֵינוּ וְעַל כָּל
יִשְׂרָאֵל, וְאִמְרוּ אָמֵן.
יְראוּ אֶת יהוה קְדֹשָׁיו, כִּי אֵין
מַחְסוֹר לִירֵאָיו : כְּפִירִים רָשׁוּ
וְרָעֵבוּ, וְדוֹרְשֵׁי יהוה לֹא יַחְסְרוּ
כָל טוֹב : הוֹדוּ לַיהוה כִּי טוֹב,
כִּי לְעוֹלָם חַסְדּוֹ : פּוֹתֵחַ אֶת יָדֶךְ
וּמַשְׂבִּיעַ לְכָל חַי רָצוֹן : בָּרוּךְ
הַגֶּבֶר אֲשֶׁר יִבְטַח בַּיהוה, וְהָיָה
יהוה מִבְטַחוֹ : נַעַר הָיִיתִי, גַּם
זָקַנְתִּי, וְלֹא רָאִיתִי צַדִּיק נֶעֱזָב
וְזַרְעוֹ מְבַקֶּשׁ־לָחֶם : יהוה עֹז
לְעַמּוֹ יִתֵּן, יהוה יְבָרֵךְ אֶת עַמּוֹ
בַשָּׁלוֹם :

to his king, and showeth mercy to his anointed, unto David and his seed for evermore" *(II Samuel 22:51).* He who makes peace in his high places, may He make peace for us and for all Israel. And let us say, Amen.

"O fear the Lord, ye his saints, for there is no want to them that fear Him. The young lions do lack, and suffer hunger, but they that seek the Lord shall not want any good thing" *(Psalm 34:9-10).* "O give thanks unto the Lord, for He is good: for His mercy endureth for ever" *(Psalm 118:1).* "Thou openest Thy hand and satisfiest the desire of every living thing" *(Psalm 145:16).* "Blessed is the man that trusteth in the Lord, and whose hope the Lord is" *(Jeremiah 17:7).* "I have been young and now am old; yet have I not seen the righteous forsaken nor his seed begging bread" *(Psalm 37:25).* "The Lord will give strength unto his people: the Lord will bless his people with peace" *(Psalm 29:11).*

At a wedding-feast, the six marriage blessings said under the *huppah* are repeated here.

Berakha Aharona

After eating cereals (except bread) or the special "fruits of the
Land of Israel" (grapes, figs, pomegranates, olives and dates),
or drinking wine, say:

בָּרוּךְ אַתָּה יהוה אֱלֹהֵינוּ מֶלֶךְ הָעוֹלָם, עַל

Blessed art Thou, O Lord our God, King of the universe

on cakes   הַמִּחְיָה וְעַל הַכַּלְכָּלָה

for the nourishment and for the sustenance

on wine   הַגֶּפֶן וְעַל פְּרִי הַגֶּפֶן

for the vine and for the fruit of the vine

on the fruits   הָעֵץ וְעַל פְּרִי הָעֵץ

for the tree and for the fruit of the tree

וְעַל תְּנוּבַת הַשָּׂדֶה וְעַל אֶרֶץ חֶמְדָּה טוֹבָה
וּרְחָבָה, שֶׁרָצִיתָ וְהִנְחַלְתָּ לַאֲבוֹתֵינוּ לֶאֱכֹל
מִפִּרְיָהּ וְלִשְׂבֹּעַ מִטּוּבָהּ. רַחֶם־נָא יהוה אֱלֹהֵינוּ
עַל יִשְׂרָאֵל עַמֶּךְ וְעַל יְרוּשָׁלַיִם עִירֶךְ וְעַל צִיּוֹן
מִשְׁכַּן כְּבוֹדֶךְ וְעַל מִזְבַּחֲךָ וְעַל הֵיכָלֶךְ. וּבְנֵה
יְרוּשָׁלַיִם עִיר הַקֹּדֶשׁ בִּמְהֵרָה בְיָמֵינוּ, וְהַעֲלֵנוּ
לְתוֹכָהּ וְשַׂמְּחֵנוּ בְּבִנְיָנָהּ וְנֹאכַל מִפִּרְיָהּ וְנִשְׂבַּע
מִטּוּבָהּ, וּנְבָרֶכְךָ עָלֶיהָ בִּקְדֻשָּׁה וּבְטָהֳרָה.

and for the produce of the field and for the lovely,
goodly and spacious land which Thou didst love and
which Thou didst give to our fathers as an inheritance,
to eat of its fruits and sate themselves on its plenty.
Have mercy, O Lord our God, on Thy people Israel, on
Jerusalem Thy city, on Zion the abode of Thy glory, on
Thy altar and on Thy Temple, and rebuild Jerusalem,
the holy city, soon, in our days. O bring us up into its
midst, that we may rejoice in its restoration and eat of
its fruits, sate ourselves on its plenty and bless Thee for
it all in holiness and purity.

On the Sabbath say: וּרְצֵה וְהַחֲלִיצֵנוּ בְּיוֹם הַשַּׁבָּת
הַזֶּה,

and be pleased to strengthen us on this Sabbath day,

On *Rosh Hodesh* say: וְזָכְרֵנוּ לְטוֹבָה בְּיוֹם רֹאשׁ
הַחֹדֶשׁ הַזֶּה,

and remember us for good on this *Rosh Hodesh* day,

On *Rosh Hashana* say: וְזָכְרֵנוּ לְטוֹבָה בְּיוֹם הַזִּכָּרוֹן
הַזֶּה,

and remember us for good on this Day of
Remembrance,

60

On the three pilgrimage festivals (Passover, *Shavuot* and *Succot*) say:

וְשַׂמְּחֵנוּ בְּיוֹם   and cause us to rejoice on this day,

On Passover say: חַג הַמַּצוֹת הַזֶּה,   the feast of *matzot*,

On *Shavuot* say: חַג הַשָּׁבוּעוֹת הַזֶּה,   the feast of *Shavuot*,

On *Succot* say: חַג הַסֻּכּוֹת הַזֶּה,   the feast of *Succot*,

On *Shemini Atseret* say: הַשְּׁמִינִי חַג הָעֲצֶרֶת הַזֶּה,   of *Shemini Atseret*,

כִּי אַתָּה יהוה טוֹב וּמֵטִיב לַכֹּל וְנוֹדֶה לְּךָ עַל הָאָרֶץ   for Thou, O Lord, art good and doest good to all, and we thank Thee for the land

on cakes

וְעַל הַמִּחְיָה. בָּרוּךְ אַתָּה יהוה, עַל הָאָרֶץ וְעַל הַמִּחְיָה.   and for the nourishment. Blessed art Thou, O Lord, for the land and for the sustenance.

on wine

וְעַל פְּרִי גַפְנָה. בָּרוּךְ אַתָּה יהוה, עַל הָאָרֶץ וְעַל פְּרִי גַפְנָה.   and for the fruit of the vine. Blessed art Thou, O Lord. for the land and for the fruit of the vine.

on the "fruits of the Land"

וְעַל פֵּירוֹתֶיהָ. בָּרוּךְ אַתָּה יהוה, עַל הָאָרֶץ וְעַל פֵּירוֹתֶיהָ.   and for its fruits. Blessed art Thou, O Lord, for the Land and for its fruits.

After food and drink following which Grace or the *Berakha Aharona* are not said, say:

בָּרוּךְ אַתָּה יהוה אֱלֹהֵינוּ מֶלֶךְ הָעוֹלָם, בּוֹרֵא נְפָשׁוֹת רַבּוֹת וְחֶסְרוֹנָן, עַל כָּל מַה שֶּׁבָּרָא לְהַחֲיוֹת בָּהֶם נֶפֶשׁ כָּל חָי. בָּרוּךְ חֵי הָעוֹלָמִים.   Blessed art Thou, O Lord our God, King of the universe, who hath created many beings with their needs, for the means Thou hast provided to sustain the life of every one of them. Blessed is He Who is the life of all the worlds.

61

וַיִּבְכּוּ בְנֵי יִשְׂרָאֵל

אֶת־מֹשֶׁה

בְּעַרְבֹת מוֹאָב

שְׁלֹשִׁים יוֹם,

וַיִּתְּמוּ יְמֵי בְכִי

אֵבֶל מֹשֶׁה:

Mourning

"And the children of Israel wept for Moses in the plains of Moab thirty days; so the days of weeping and mourning for Moses were ended."

(Deuteronomy 34:8)

It is a commandment of the Torah to mourn the death of a member of the immediate family. With regard to mourning, seven members are considered to be "immediate" relations: a father, a mother, a brother, a sister, a son, a daughter and a spouse. Just as the intensity of the sorrow diminishes with the passage of time from the moment of death, so, with the passage of time, the rules of mourning become less severe. The rules of mourning begin to apply only after the burial of the deceased person. From the moment of death until after the burial the mourner is called *onen*, and out of respect for the unburied deceased one, the mourner is exempt from all the "Thou shalt" commandments of the Torah.

Some of the Mourning Rites

As soon as one learns about the death of an "immediate" relation, one rends one's clothes.

The rules of mourning become effective immediately after the burial. The mourner must then take off his or her leather shoes.

After the funeral, on their way out of the cemetery, the mourners pass between two rows of people who accompanied the deceased, and the latter console the mourners, saying:

"הַמָּקוֹם יְנַחֵם אוֹתְךָ (אֶתְכֶם) בְּתוֹךְ שְׁאָר אֲבֵלֵי צִיּוֹן וִירוּשָׁלָיִם".

May the Lord comfort you among the mourners for Zion and Jerusalem.

On the way out of the cemetery, those who have been
present at the burial wash their hands and say:

בִּלַּע הַמָּוֶת לָנֶצַח״
וּמָחָה אֲדֹנָי יֱהֹוִה
דִּמְעָה מֵעַל כָּל־פָּנִים,
וְחֶרְפַּת עַמּוֹ יָסִיר
מֵעַל כָּל־הָאָרֶץ
כִּי יהוה דִּבֵּר״.

He will swallow up death for ever,
And the Lord God will wipe away
Tears from all faces,
And the reproach of His people he will remove
From all the earth;
For the Lord has spoken.   *(Isaiah 25:8)*

The mourning is heaviest during the first
seven days after the burial. During that time
the mourner does no work and does not leave
his house (except on the Sabbath when, in
public, the rules of mourning do not apply).
For that reason, during these seven days a
minyan for prayer assembles in the mourner's
house. Also, the mourner does not wear
leather shoes, shave or cut his hair. In all the
prayer services, the mourner says the *kaddish*,
which is essentially an affirmation of the
greatness of God. After the seven days have
elapsed and until thirty days after the funeral,
the rules of mourning grow less stringent, but
the mourner still says *kaddish* in the
synagogue and does not shave or cut his hair.
When one of his parents dies, a son says
kaddish until the end of eleven months after
the burial. He must conduct himself with
gravity until a year after the burial and not
participate in festivities or wear new clothes.

Comforting the Mourners

The custom of sitting in one's house for seven days after the funeral is know as "sitting *shiv'a*" — *shiv'a* meaning seven. During that period, one should visit the mourner and speak words of consolation. The mourner sits on a low stool close to the ground. One should take care not to act frivolously in the house of mourning and to converse little of mundane matters. One does not give the greeting *"Shalom,"* and on leaving one says:

"הַמָּקוֹם יְנַחֵם אוֹתְךָ (אֶתְכֶם) בְּתוֹךְ שְׁאָר אֲבֵלֵי צִיוֹן וִירוּשָׁלָיִם".

May the Lord comfort you among the mourners of Zion and Jerusalem.

Mourner's Kaddish

The mourner:

יִתְגַּדַּל וְיִתְקַדַּשׁ שְׁמֵהּ רַבָּא

Magnified and sanctified be His great name.

The congregation responds:

אָמֵן.

Amen.

The mourner:

בְּעָלְמָא דִי בְרָא כִרְעוּתֵהּ, וְיַמְלִיךְ מַלְכוּתֵהּ בְּחַיֵּיכוֹן וּבְיוֹמֵיכוֹן וּבְחַיֵּי דְכָל בֵּית יִשְׂרָאֵל בַּעֲגָלָא וּבִזְמַן קָרִיב, וְאִמְרוּ אָמֵן.

In the world which He has created
According to His will.
May His kingdom be established in your lifetime and during your days,
And in the lifetime of all the house of Israel,
Speedily and at a near time,
And say ye, Amen.

אָמֵן. יְהֵא שְׁמֵהּ רַבָּא
מְבָרַךְ לְעָלַם וּלְעָלְמֵי עָלְמַיָּא.

Amen. May His great name
Be blessed for ever and ever.

The mourner:

יְהֵא שְׁמֵהּ רַבָּא
מְבָרַךְ לְעָלַם וּלְעָלְמֵי עָלְמַיָּא.
יִתְבָּרַךְ וְיִשְׁתַּבַּח וְיִתְפָּאַר וְיִתְרוֹמַם
וְיִתְנַשֵּׂא וְיִתְהַדָּר וְיִתְעַלֶּה וְיִתְהַלָּל
שְׁמֵהּ דְּקֻדְשָׁא, בְּרִיךְ הוּא.

May His great name
Be blessed for ever and ever.
Blessed, praised and glorified, exalted,
Extolled and honoured, magnified and lauded,
Be the name of the Holy One, Blessed be He.

בְּרִיךְ הוּא.

Blessed be He.

לְעֵלָּא (בעשרת ימי תשובה מוסיף: וּלְעֵלָּא)
מִן כָּל בִּרְכָתָא וְשִׁירָתָא,
תֻּשְׁבְּחָתָא וְנֶחֱמָתָא
דַּאֲמִירָן בְּעָלְמָא,
וְאִמְרוּ אָמֵן.

Far above
All the blessings and hymns,
Praises and consolations
That are spoken in the world,
And say ye, Amen.

> *A consideration of the day of our death gives rise to thoughts of a positive and earnest nature. "It is better to go to the house of mourning than to go to the house of feasting, for that is the end of all men, and the living shall lay it to his heart." (Ecclesiastes 7:2)*

The congregation responds: אָמֵן. Amen.

The mourner:

יְהֵא שְׁלָמָא רַבָּא מִן שְׁמַיָּא וְחַיִּים
עָלֵינוּ וְעַל כָּל יִשְׂרָאֵל,
וְאִמְרוּ אָמֵן.

May there be abundant peace from heaven and life
Upon us and upon all Israel,
And say ye, Amen.

The congregation responds: אָמֵן. Amen.

The mourner takes three steps backwards, and says:

עֹשֶׂה שָׁלוֹם בִּמְרוֹמָיו,
הוּא יַעֲשֶׂה שָׁלוֹם
עָלֵינוּ וְעַל כָּל יִשְׂרָאֵל,
וְאִמְרוּ אָמֵן.

He who makes peace in His high places,
May He make peace
Upon us and upon all Israel;
And say ye, Amen.

The congregation responds: אָמֵן.

There is a "time to be born, and a time to die."
(Ecclesiastes 3:2) Happy is the man whose hour of
death is as the hour of his birth — in that he is clean
of transgressions.

List of Illustrations